Learning to Read, Step by Step!

Ready to Read   Preschool–Kindergarten
• big type and easy words • rhyme and rhythm • picture clues
For children who know the alphabet and are eager to begin reading.

Reading with Help   Preschool–Grade 1
• basic vocabulary • short sentences • simple stories
For children who recognize familiar words and sound out new words with help.

Reading on Your Own   Grades 1–3
• engaging characters • easy-to-follow plots • popular topics
For children who are ready to read on their own.

Reading Paragraphs   Grades 2–3
• challenging vocabulary • short paragraphs • exciting stories
For newly independent readers who read simple sentences with confidence.

Ready for Chapters   Grades 2–4
• chapters • longer paragraphs • full-color art
For children who want to take the plunge into chapter books but still like colorful pictures.

STEP INTO READING® is designed to give every child a successful reading experience. The grade levels are only guides; children will progress through the steps at their own speed, developing confidence in their reading. The F&P Text Level on the back cover serves as another tool to help you choose the right book for your child.

Remember, a lifetime love of reading starts with a single step!

*For my brother, Chip, who always stands up
for what he believes —A.J.P.*

*To Jackie Robinson,
for breaking the barrier —R.C.*

Text copyright © 2008 by April Jones Prince
Cover art and interior illustrations copyright © 2008 by Robert Casilla

All rights reserved. Published in the United States by Random House Children's Books, a division of Penguin Random House LLC, New York.

Step into Reading, Random House, and the Random House colophon are registered trademarks of Penguin Random House LLC.

Photograph credits: p. 3: © MLB Photos via Getty Images; p. 6: © Bettmann/CORBIS; p. 18: © Associated Press; p. 27: © Associated Press; p. 28: © Associated Press; p. 41: © Bettmann/CORBIS; p. 44: © Associated Press; p. 45: © Associated Press; p. 46: © Associated Press; p. 47: © Associated Press; p. 48: © Bettmann/CORBIS.

Visit us on the Web!
StepIntoReading.com
rhcbooks.com

Educators and librarians, for a variety of teaching tools, visit us at
RHTeachersLibrarians.com

Library of Congress Cataloging-in-Publication Data is available upon request.
ISBN 978-0-593-43270-9 (trade) — ISBN 978-0-593-43271-6 (lib. bdg.)

Printed in the United States of America
10 9 8 7 6 5 4 3 2 1

This book has been officially leveled by using the F&P Text Level Gradient™ Leveling System.

JACKIE ROBINSON
He Led the Way

by April Jones Prince
illustrations by Robert Casilla

Random House 🏠 New York

Jack Roosevelt Robinson

was born in a small cabin

in Georgia in 1919.

Everyone called him "Jackie."

His family lived and worked

on a white man's farm.

Slavery had ended more than

50 years before.

But often, it did not seem that way.

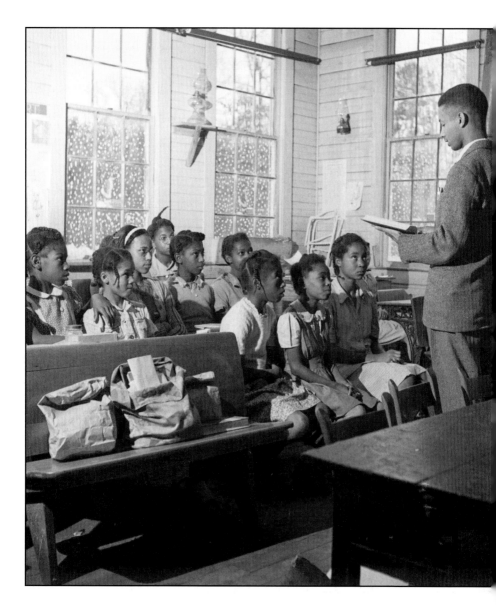

Black children could not go to school
with white children.

Black families could not eat in restaurants with white people or stay at the same hotels.

They had to sit in the back
of public buses . . .

. . . and in the worst seats
at ballparks.

One day, Jackie Robinson
would help change all this.
He did it through baseball.

Jackie's family moved to
Pasadena, California,
when he was still a small boy.

They were the only black
family on their block.
And their neighbors
did not welcome them.

But Jackie's mother told her children,
"We have the same right
to live here as anyone else."
She did not want her children
looking for trouble.
But she did want them
to stick up for themselves.

One day, a girl called
Jackie mean names.
Her father threw stones at Jackie.
What did Jackie do?
He shouted names and threw stones
right back at them.

In school, Jackie did okay.

But in sports, he made magic!

Jackie always played to win—

even a game of tag.

Kids even paid Jackie

to be on their team.

All through high school and college,
Jackie played sports:

football,

baseball,

and basketball.

He set a new record for the long jump.

He was a local hero.

His name was always in the papers.

After college, Jackie wanted to play
sports for a living.

But no major team in any sport
hired black players.

There were all-black baseball teams
like the Kansas City Monarchs
and the Homestead Grays.

These teams had their own leagues.
Fans flocked to see stars like
Satchel Paige and Josh Gibson.
The games were fast-paced
and exciting.
Jackie could play on one
of these teams . . .

. . . except for one thing:
World War II had started.
Even in the US Army,
black soldiers did not eat, sleep,
or train with white soldiers.

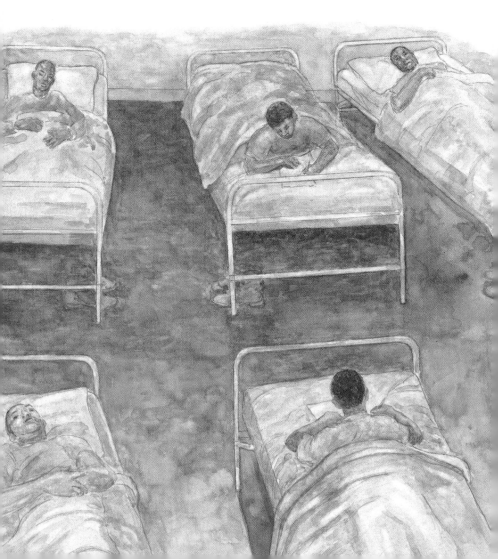

In the snack bar, only a few seats
were set aside for black soldiers.
"We are all in this war together,"
Jackie told the general.
"And everyone should have the
same rights."

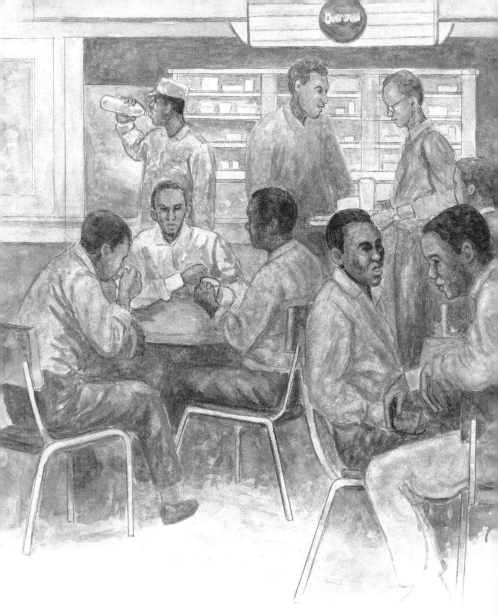

The general agreed.

Black soldiers got more seats

in the snack bar.

After the war, Jackie played baseball
for the Kansas City Monarchs.
But Jackie wasn't a Monarch for long.

Branch Rickey was the president
of the Brooklyn Dodgers.
He had heard about Jackie Robinson
from a scout named Clyde Sukeforth.
Just like Jackie, Branch Rickey
hated to lose.
He wanted to win a World Series.
There were so many
talented black ballplayers.
Rickey thought it was time that
one of them joined the Dodgers.
Maybe Jackie Robinson.

Branch Rickey asked
Jackie Robinson
to meet him in New York.
"I want you to play
for the Dodgers,"
he told Jackie.
"You will be put down
and spit upon.
But you must not fight back!
That will make people say
that blacks don't belong
in the major leagues.
Do you have the guts to play
no matter what?"

It was not Jackie Robinson's nature
to keep quiet.
But he decided he had to.
He gave Branch Rickey his answer:
"YES."

In 1946, Jackie married
his college sweetheart, Rachel Isum.
She traveled with him to
spring training in Florida.

Jackie played his first season
on a Dodgers minor-league team.
This was like practice for
the major leagues.
As always, he played to win.
He led his league in hitting
and was tied in runs scored.
He was second in stolen bases.

So on April 15, 1947,
Jackie Robinson made history
as the first black ballplayer
in the major leagues.
He stepped onto Ebbets Field
in Brooklyn.

He was wearing a Dodgers uniform.

He was their new first baseman.

He said it was a dream come true.

Branch Rickey's warning

also came true.

Once again, people called

Jackie mean names.

He got hateful letters.

At games, pitchers on the other team

threw balls at his head on purpose.

Even many of the Dodgers
did not want him around.
Jackie took it all in silence.

But lots of fans adored Jackie
right from the start.

GO
JACKIE

His courage and flashy play
proved that black players
belonged in the major leagues.
Jackie hit and ran as well as
the best of his white teammates.

But he had a way of stealing bases
that was all his own.
Jackie could even steal
home plate!

He would dance
on and off third base.
Then he'd dart down
the baseline.
The next moment,
he was sliding into home plate.
Score!
Jackie was named Rookie of the Year.

By 1949, Jackie had been
quiet long enough.

Now he spoke up when
umpires made bad calls.

And he talked back
to ballplayers
on other teams.
Jackie lost some fans.
But he was standing up
for his rights—
not just in baseball,
but in all of America.
In 1949, he was voted
the National League's
Most Valuable Player.
It was a great honor.
Jackie deserved it.

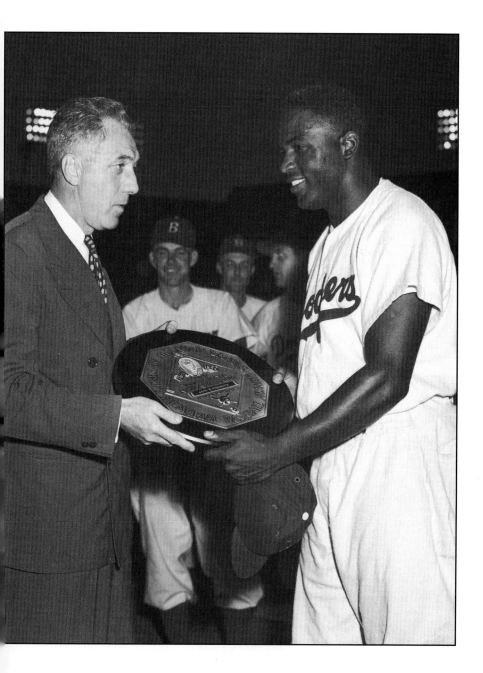

Jackie helped the Dodgers
get to the World Series six times.
Five times, they lost.
Then, in 1955,
they finally won!
Jackie said the win was
"one of the greatest thrills
of my life."

By that time, there were almost 40 black players on major-league teams. There were black players in other pro sports, too.

Roy Campanella

Jackie Robinson had
helped change America.

Willie Mays   Hank Aaron

Jackie played in the major leagues
for 10 years.

Then he became a businessman.

He spent more time with Rachel
and their three children.

And he kept working for

equal rights.

In 1962, Jackie was the first black
man voted into the Baseball Hall
of Fame.

Jackie lived to be 53.

He showed America that talent is not
based on skin color.

Jackie Robinson was a great
ballplayer—and a great American.